WHY YOUR CAT THINKS YOU'RE AN IDIOT

the hilarious
guide to all
the ways
your cat is
judging you

SAM HART

ILLUSTRATED BY **FIN KENDALL**

CONGRATULATIONS, YOU'VE MADE ONE OF LIFE'S MOST IMPORTANT DECISIONS:

YOU'VE REALIZED YOU'RE A CAT-PERSON!

Your sole purpose in life is to dote upon your cat. You happily provide every tummy tickle, bag of treats and head-scratch they demand. And what do you seem to get in return? Judgmental looks, a turned-up nose, or even worse: they completely ignore you.

Now, you might be wondering why your precious, pampered puss doesn't quite share your boundless enthusiasm. In fact, they're treating you like you can't even master the alphabet!

But please, don't take it personally – just let your cat explain the many different reasons why they think you're an idiot!

A human can
live with us for
years and yet
fail to learn even
the basics of
our language.

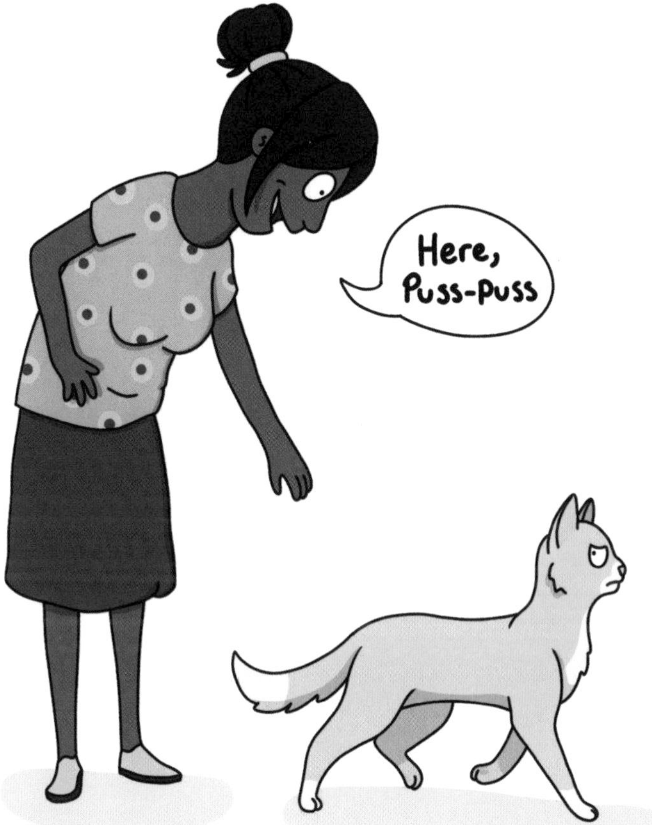
Here, Puss-puss

Humans insist on total privacy when they poop. It's like it's top secret, or something.

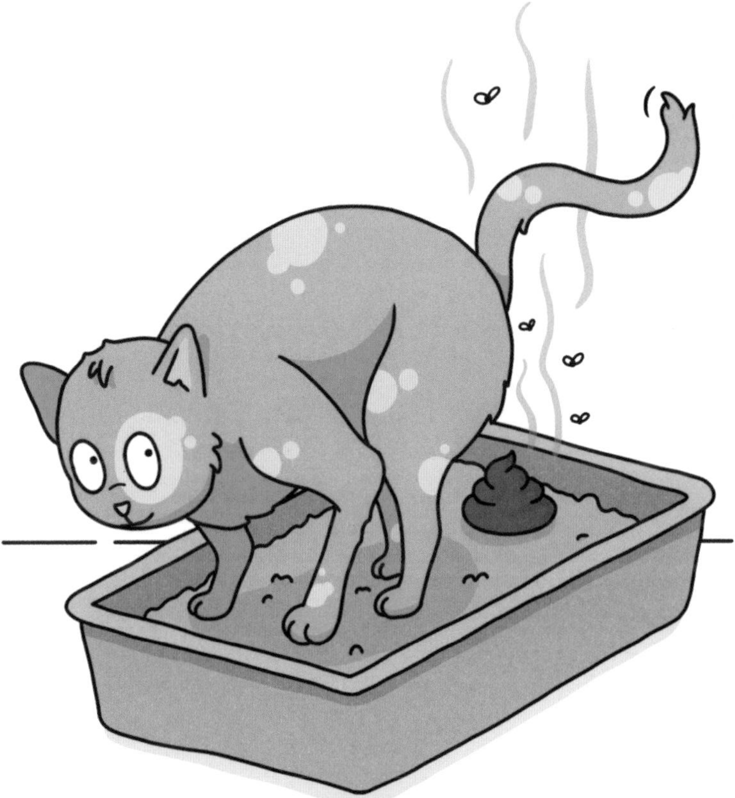

Why do they feel
the need to label
all their items?
What's wrong
with "spray it,
don't say it"?

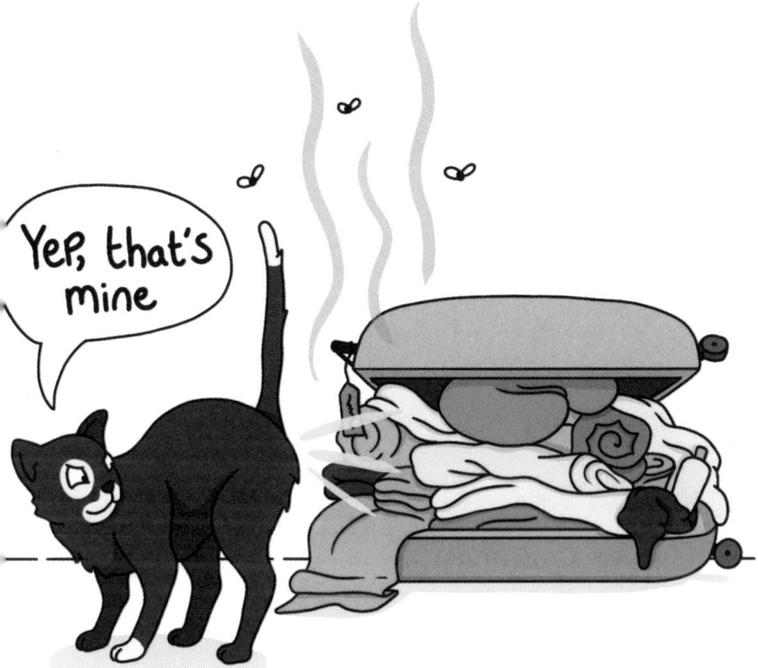
Yep, that's mine

They get so
excited when
their parcel
arrives, only
to throw away
the best part!

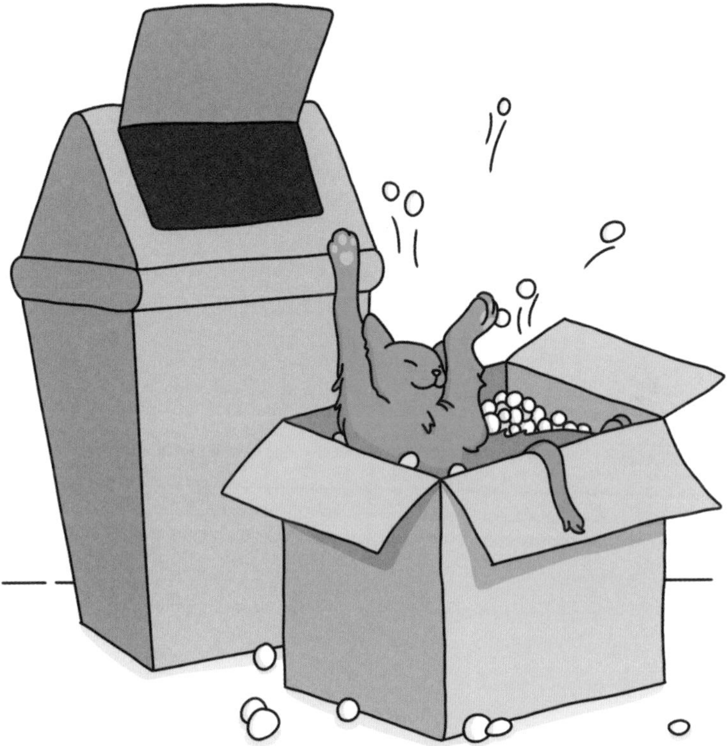

We know we're
gorgeous, but
they can't
seriously expect
us to be camera-
ready every
second of the day.

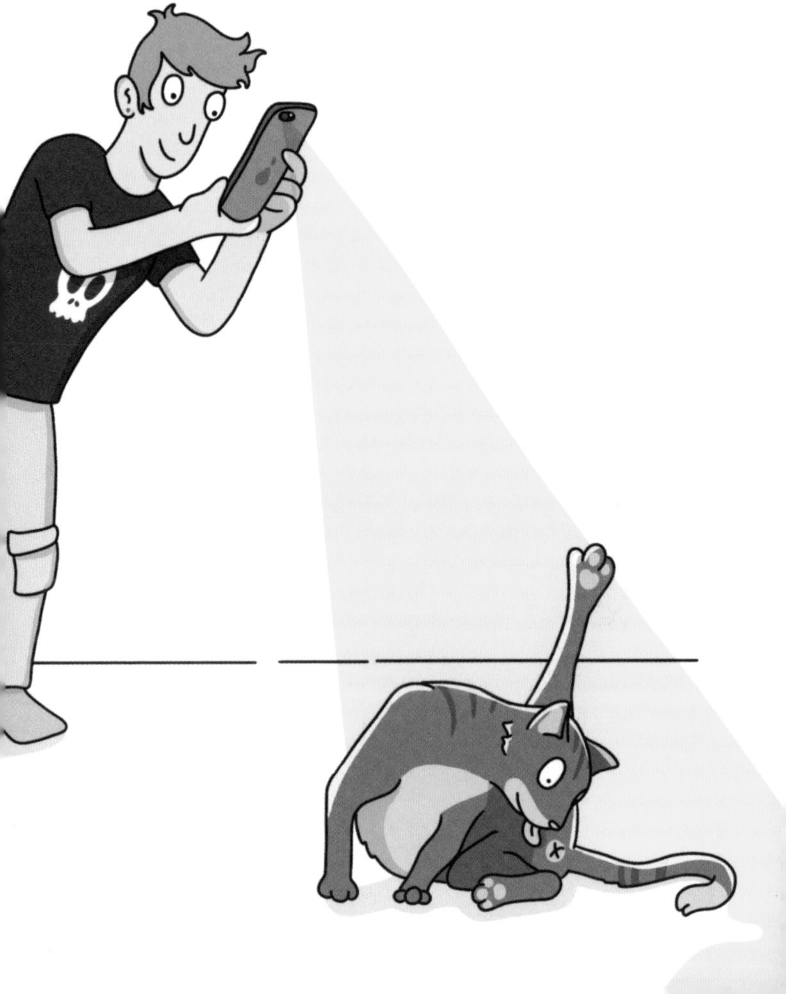

What is the point
of the big noisy
screen when
they're always on
the little one?

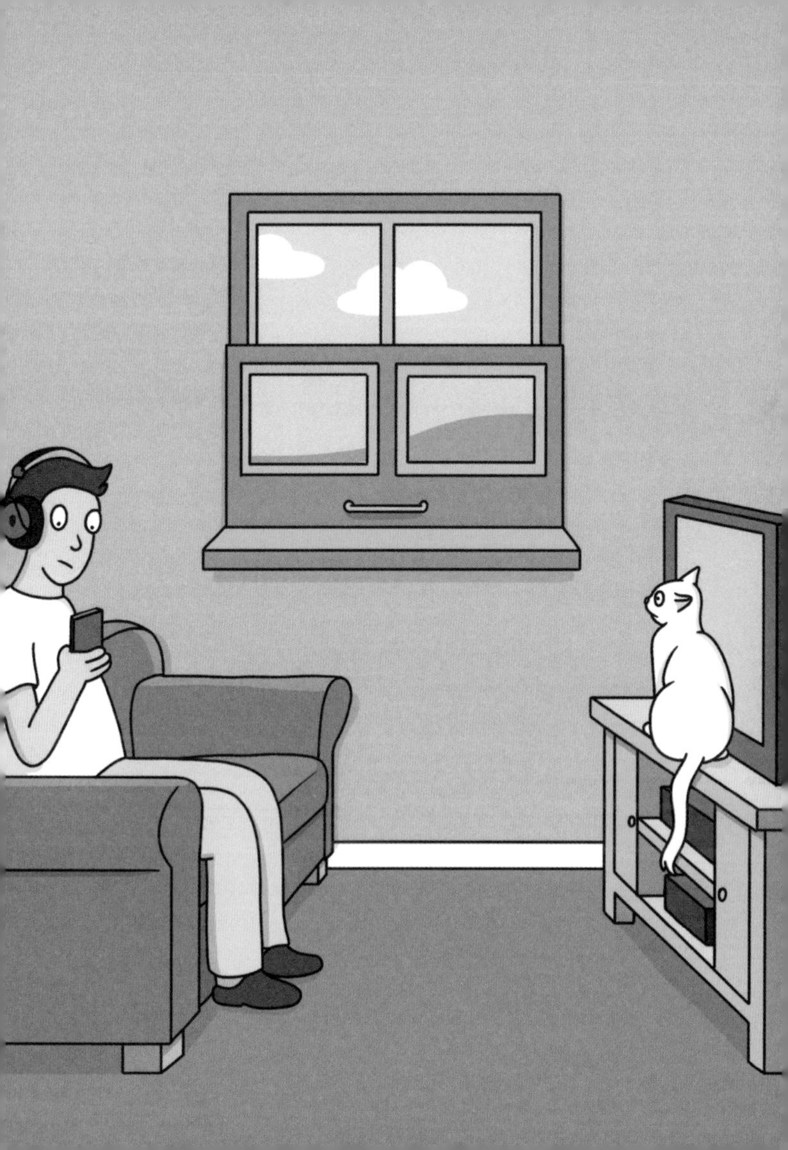

If you leave your valuables so close to the edge, then you're *asking* for trouble.

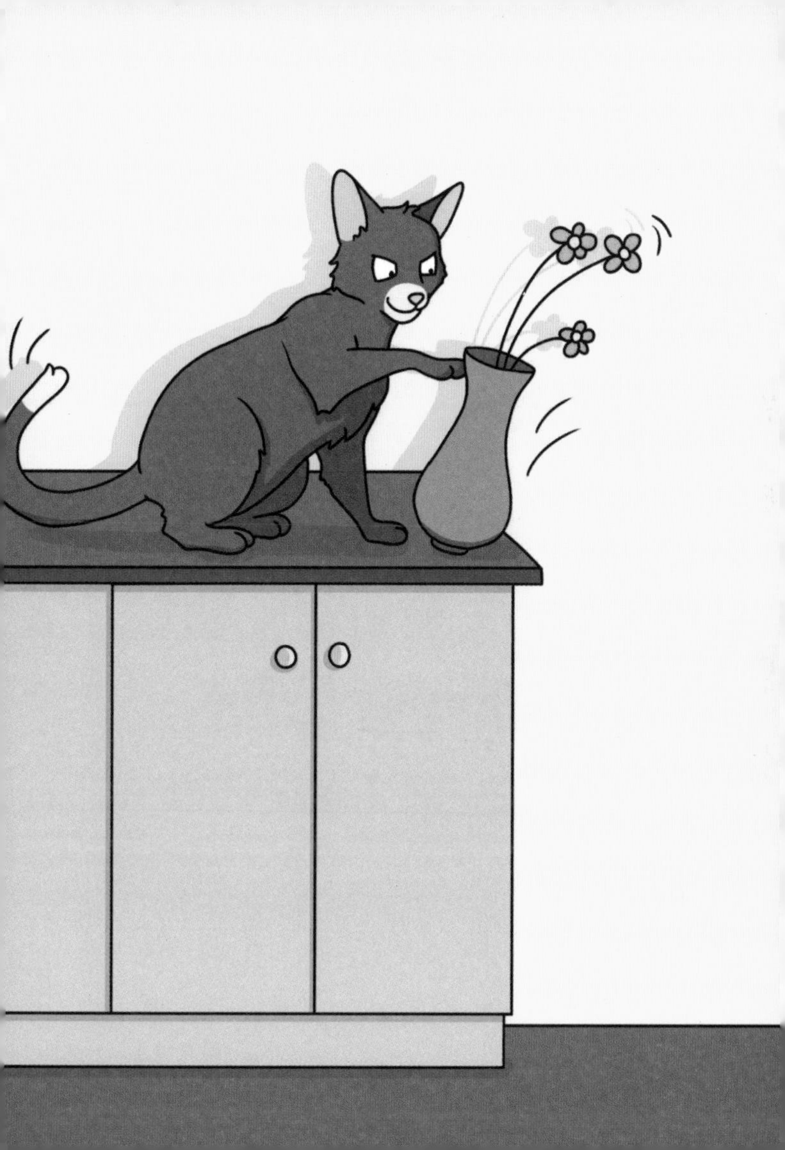

It puzzles us
that they still
don't know what
a mouse is for.

They make a
humiliating fuss
of us every 12
months and we
have no idea why.

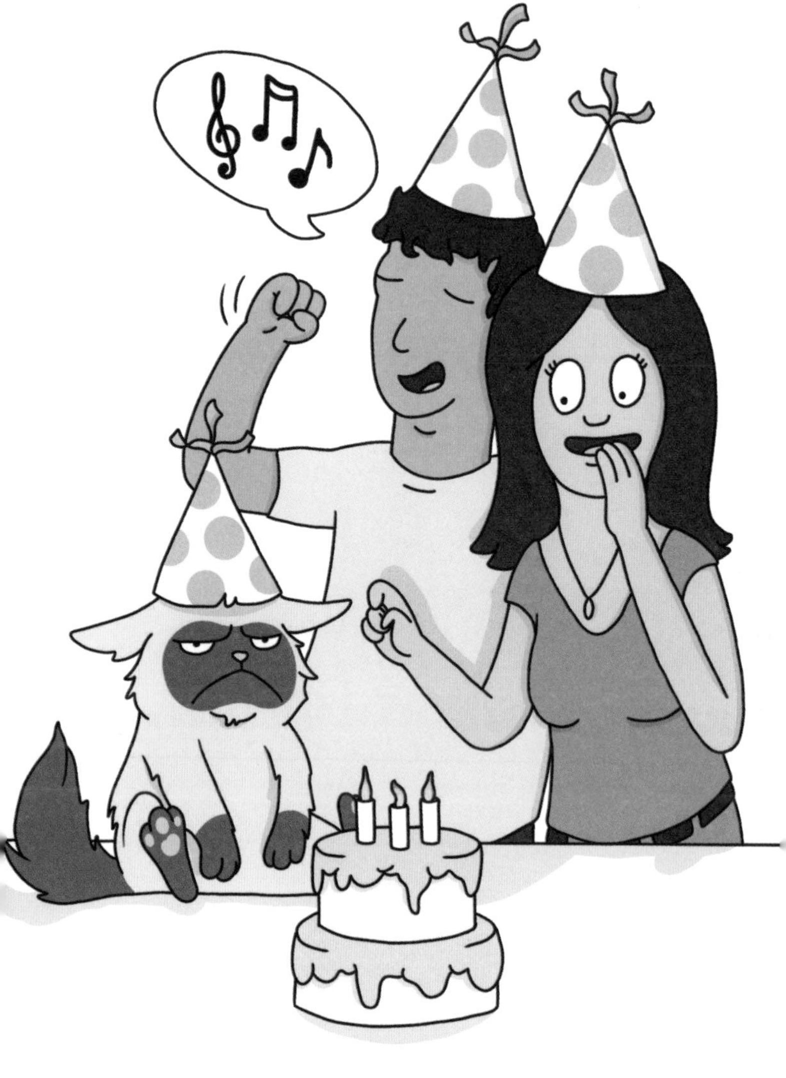

Can you imagine coughing for all that time and having nothing to show for it?

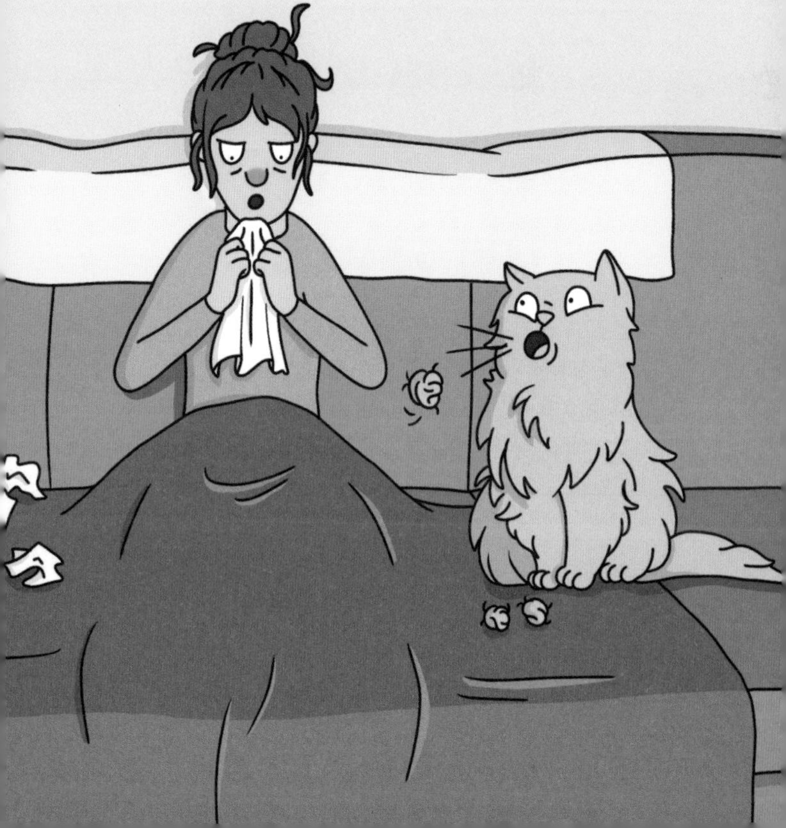

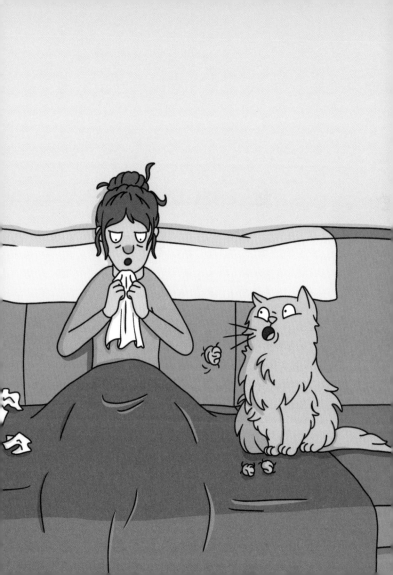

You wouldn't
believe we inspired
the catwalk.
This is a crime
against fashion.

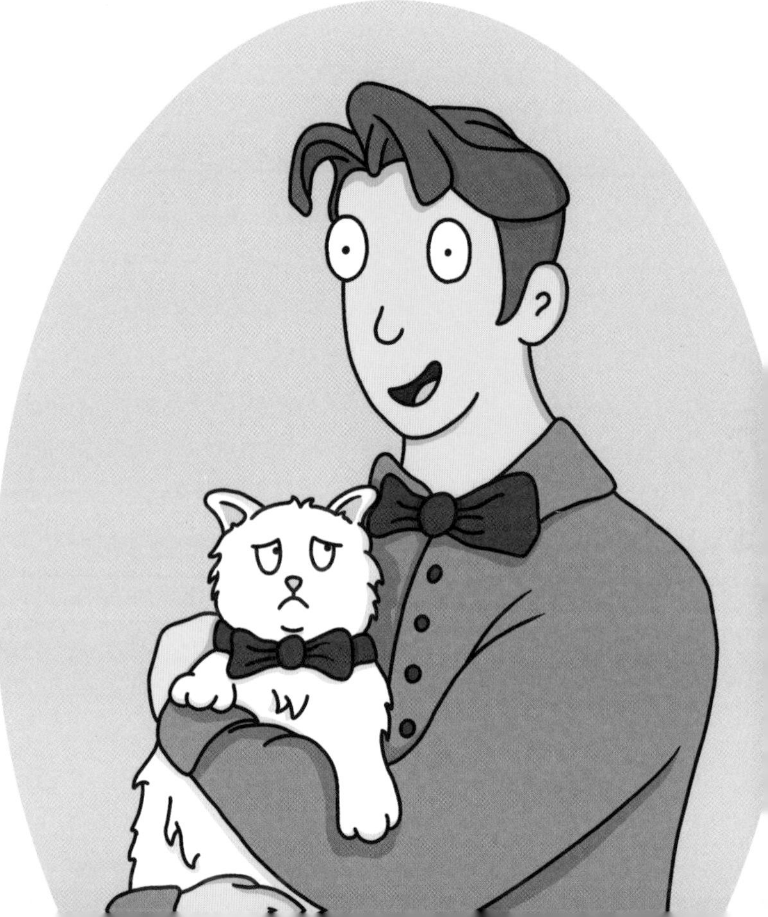

They love to sing to us, but they hate it when we serenade them.

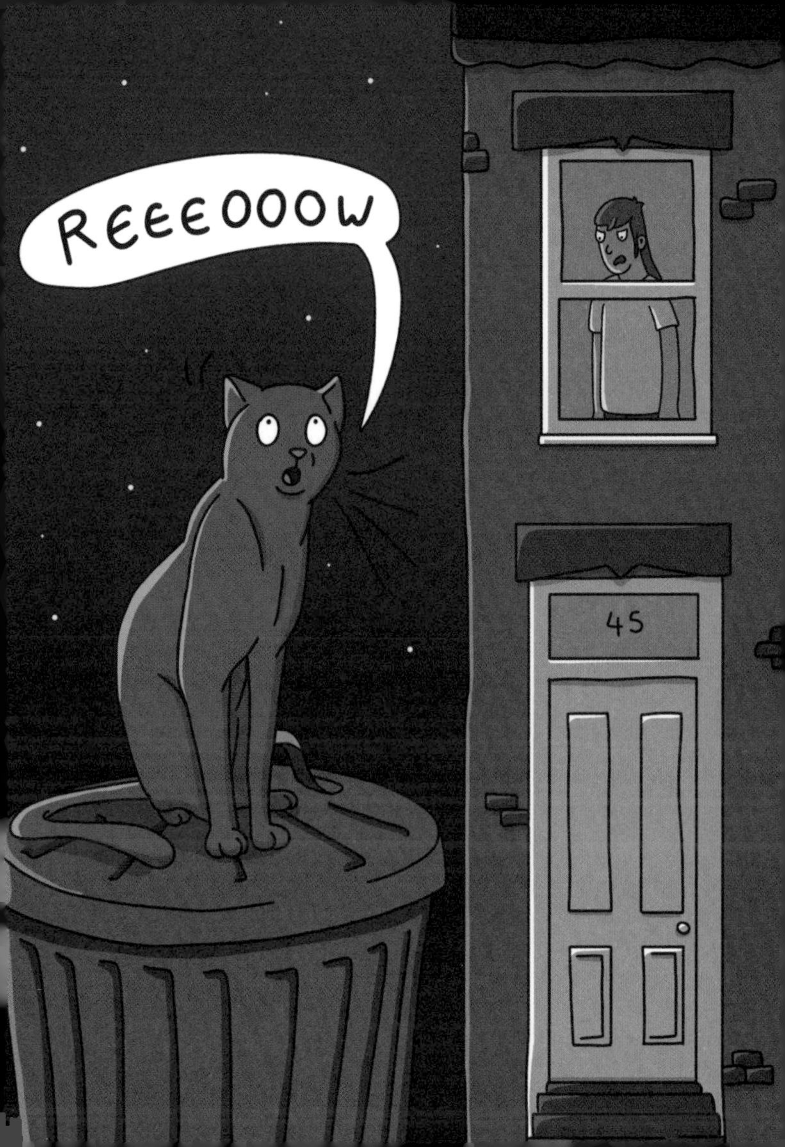
REEEOOOW
45

It is impossible not
to be suspicious
of anyone who
only eats three
meals a day.

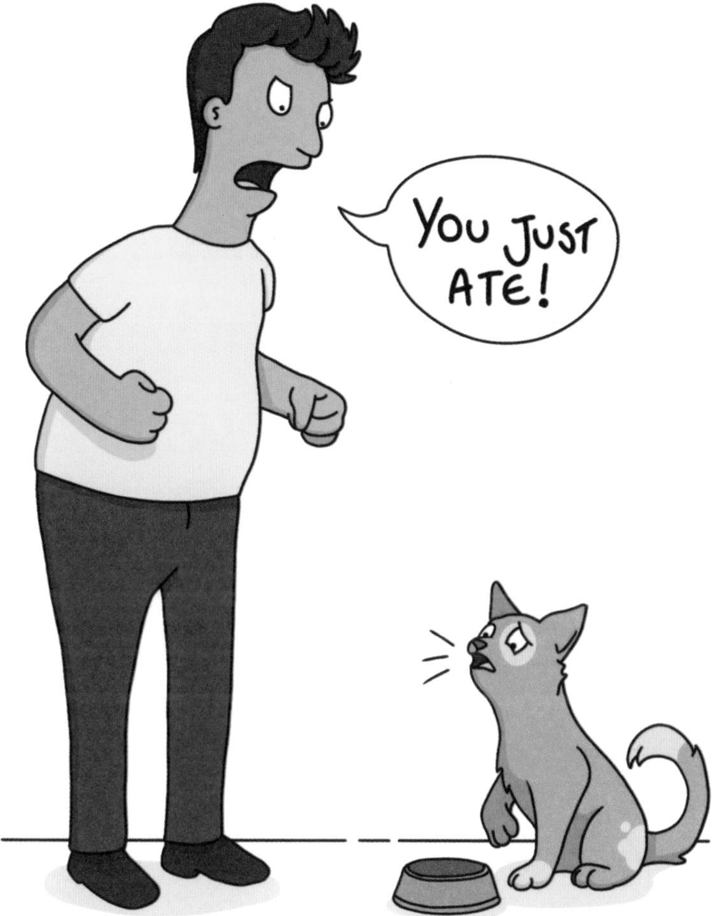
YOU JUST ATE!

They just don't know when to stop, do they?

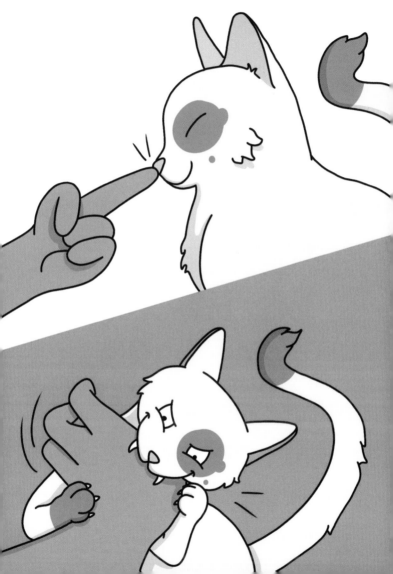

They should
schedule their
toilet breaks more
considerately.

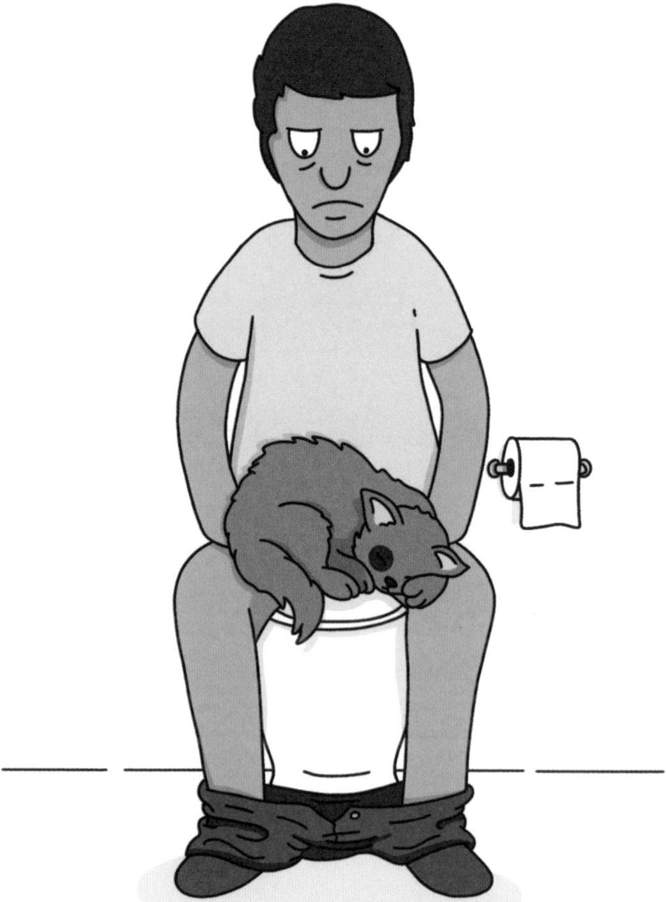

Why is it always
our fault when
they can't meet
their deadlines?

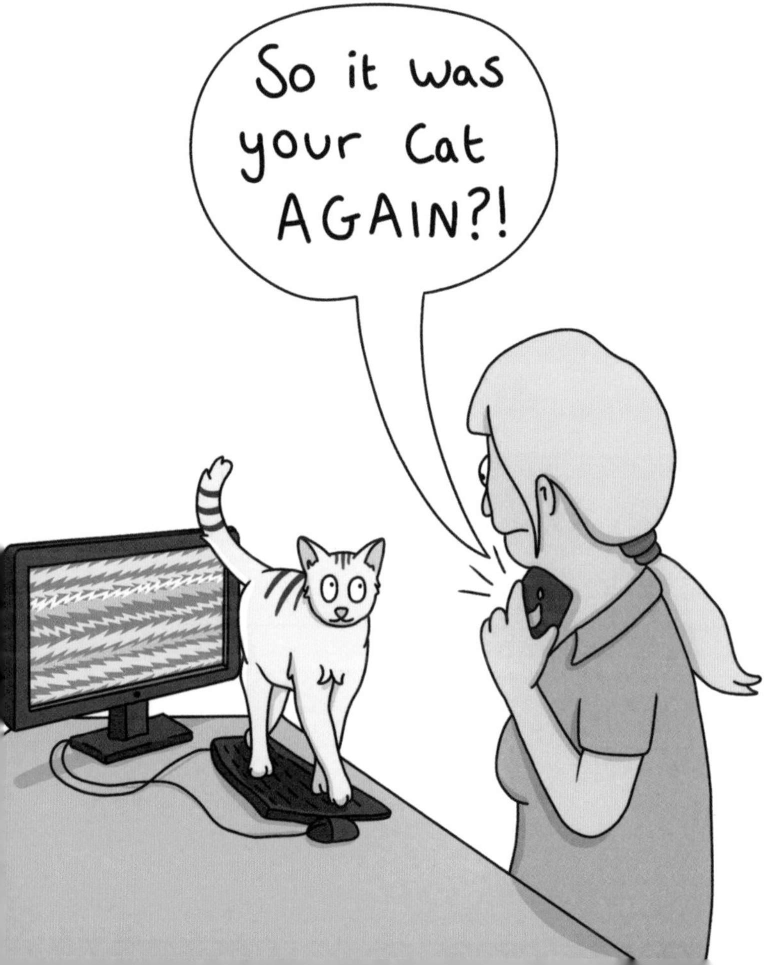
So it was your Cat AGAIN?!

There's a reason why cat burglars are so much smarter than human ones.

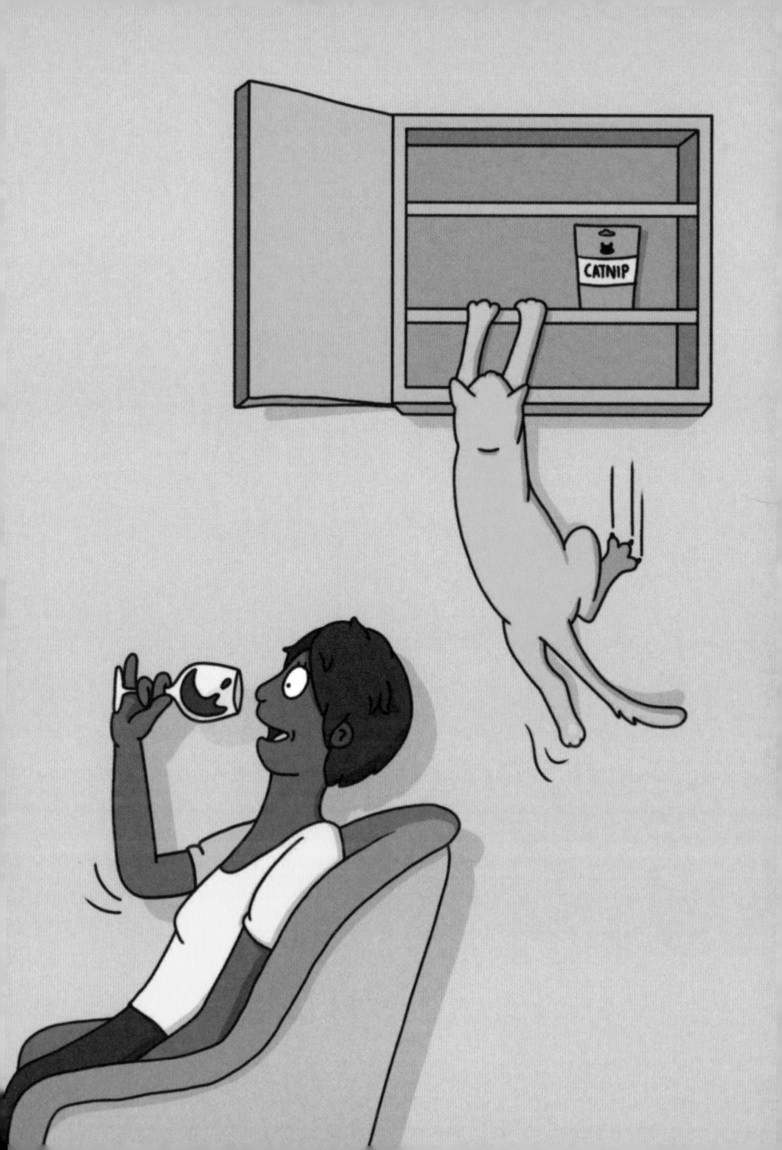
CATNIP

They're so easily impressed by their species' physical feats.

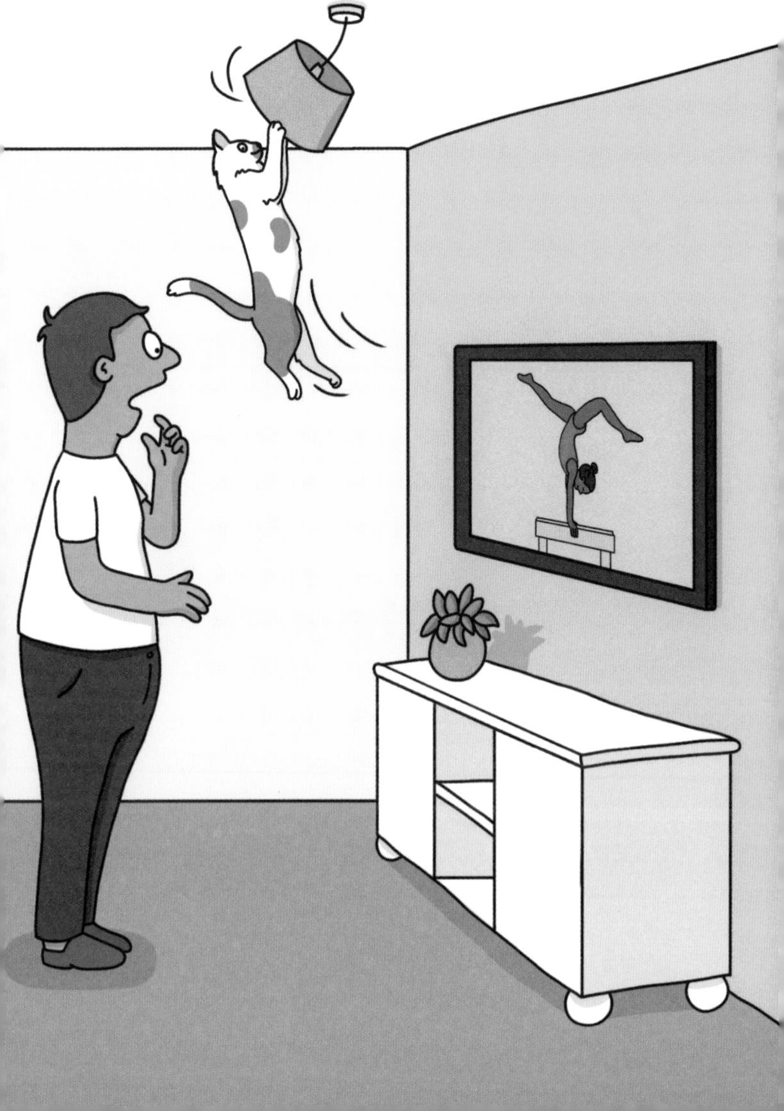

They expect a hero's welcome every time they walk through the door.

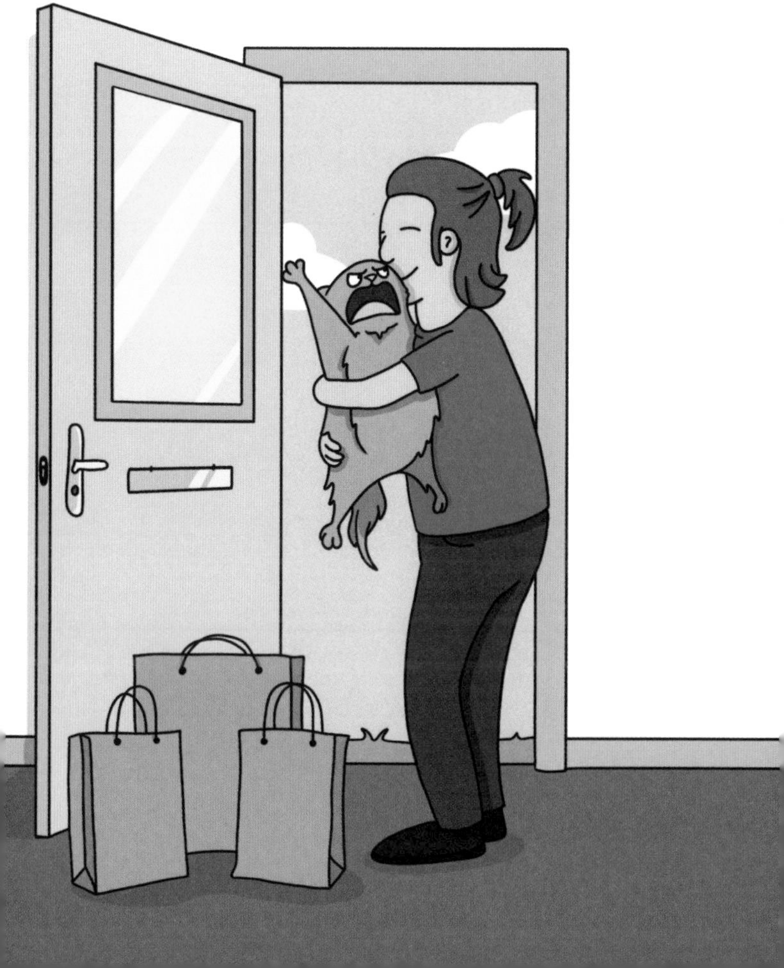

We will never
understand how
they can find a
bath relaxing.

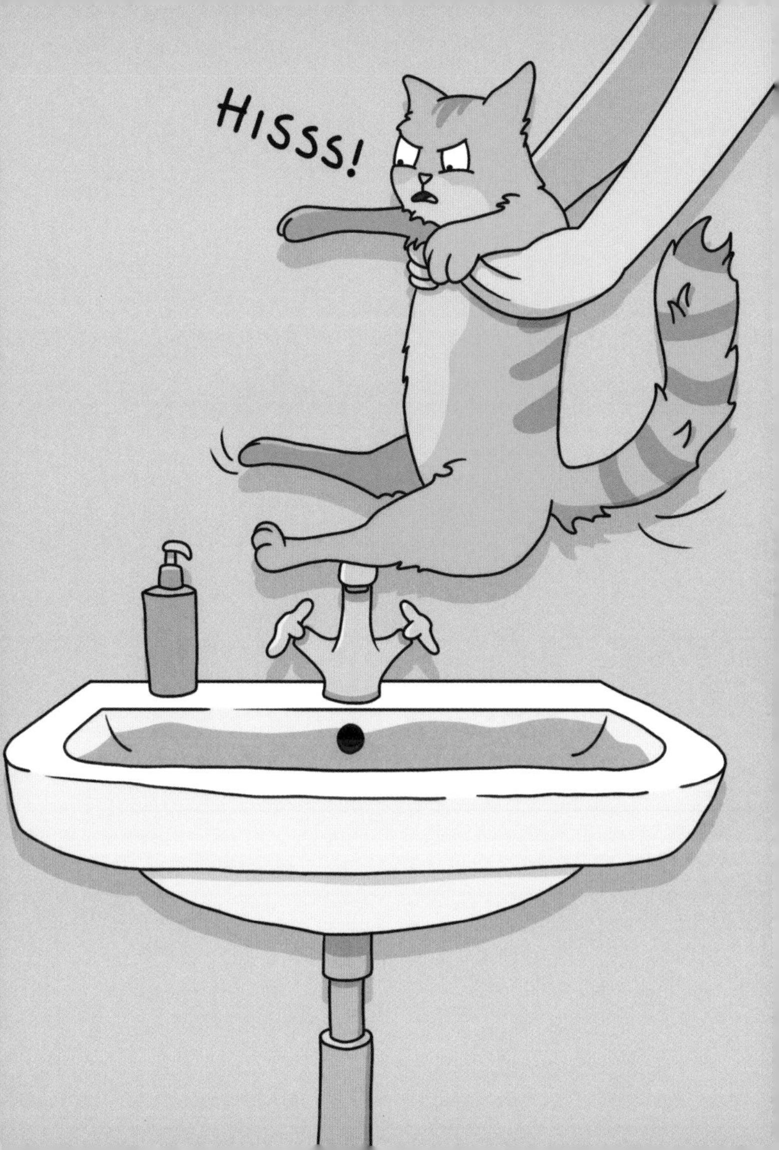
HISSS!

They make
themselves
hairless and then
complain that
they're cold.

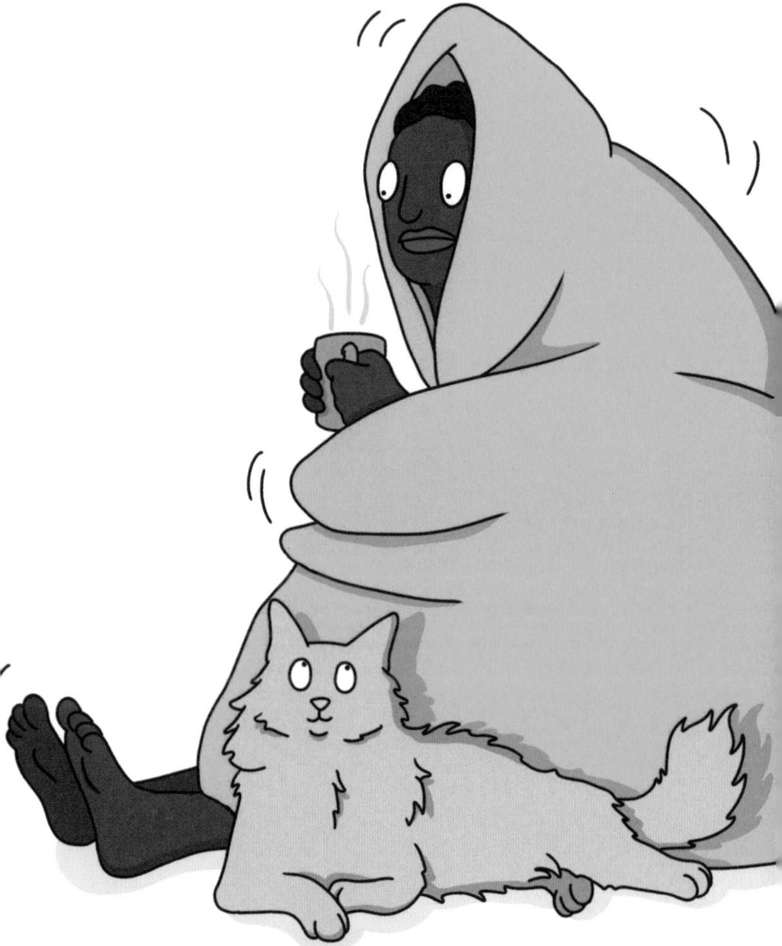

When will they
learn that we
do *not* respond
well to bribery?

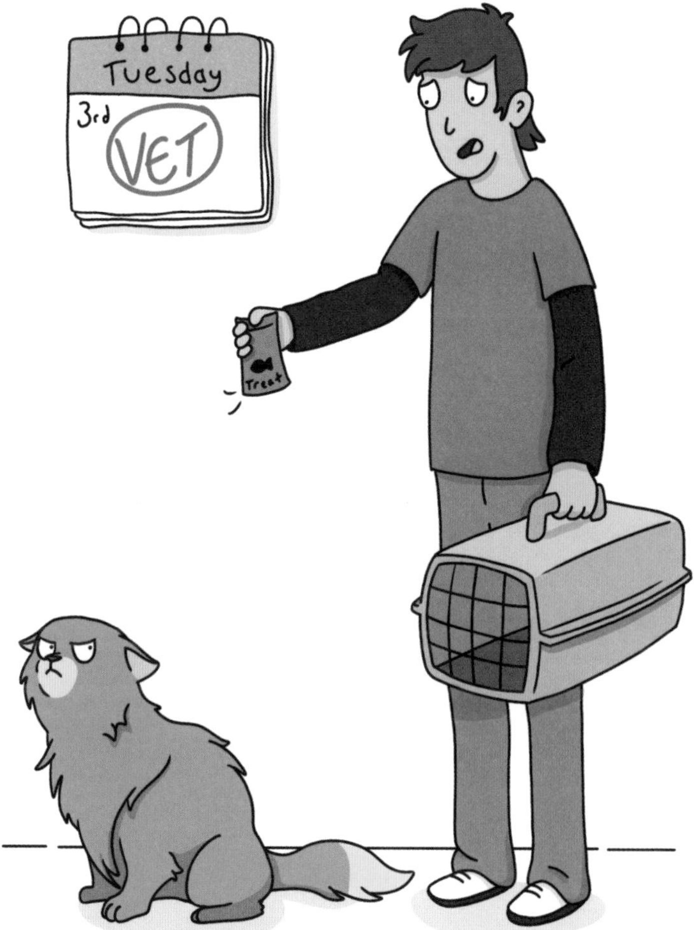
Tuesday
3rd
VET
Treat

Despite all their online tutorials, we *still* have to show them how to do yoga properly.

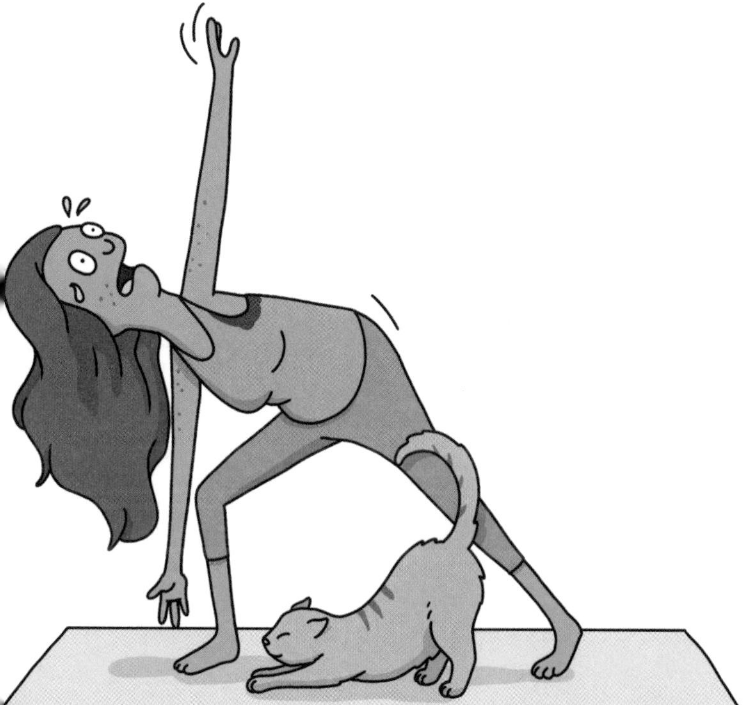

For all their talk
of how much we
mean to them,
sometimes
they make us
feel completely
overlooked.

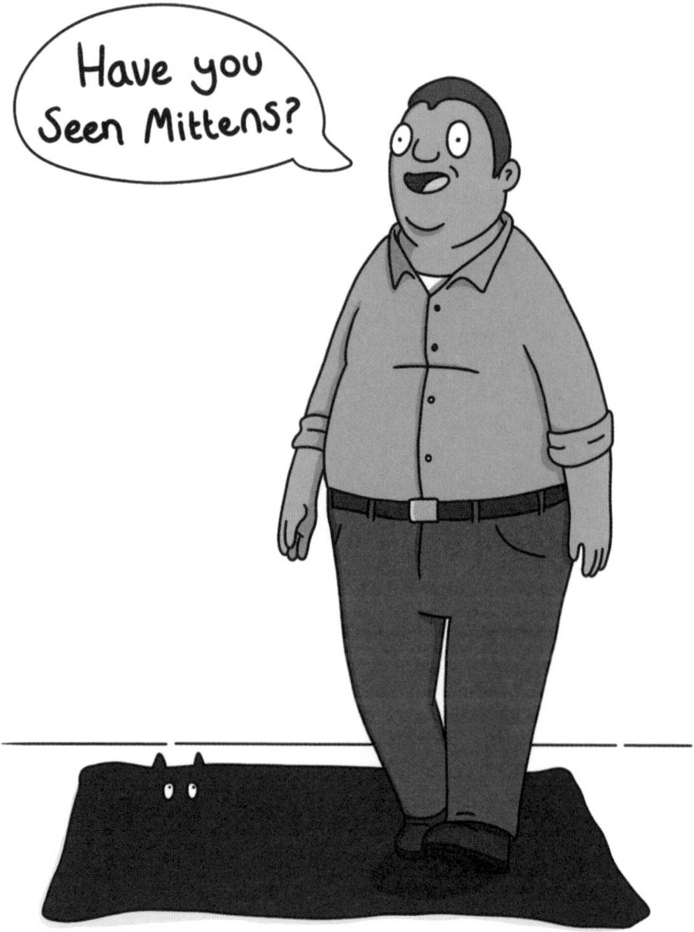
Have you Seen Mittens?

Their sayings
make absolutely
no sense!

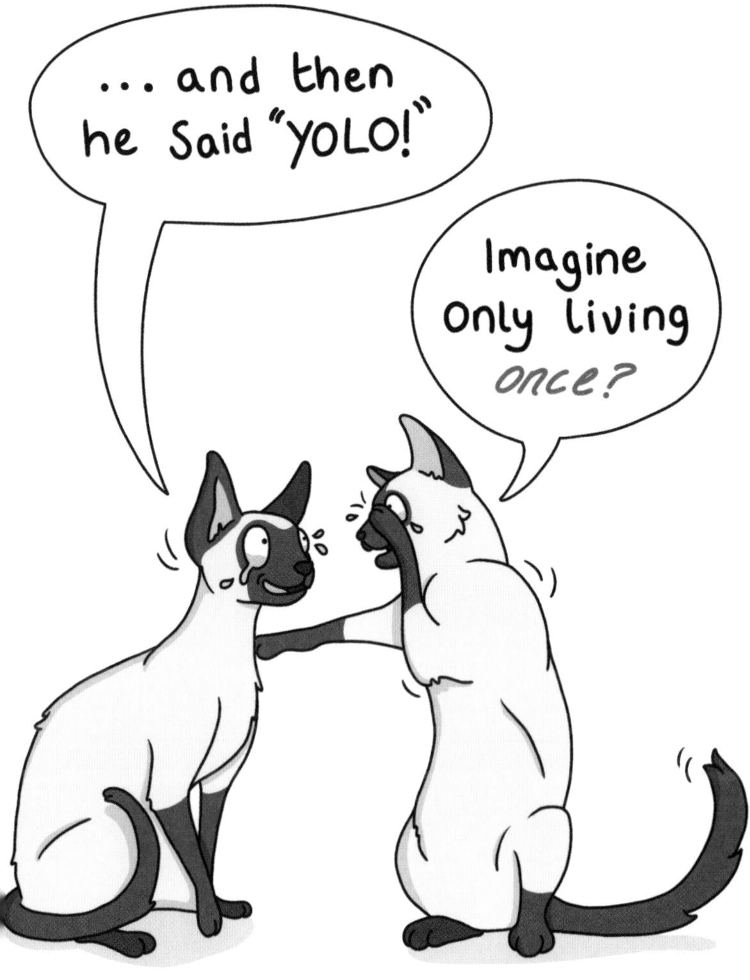
... and then he Said "YOLO!"
Imagine Only living once?

They act as though they've never seen a contortionist before.

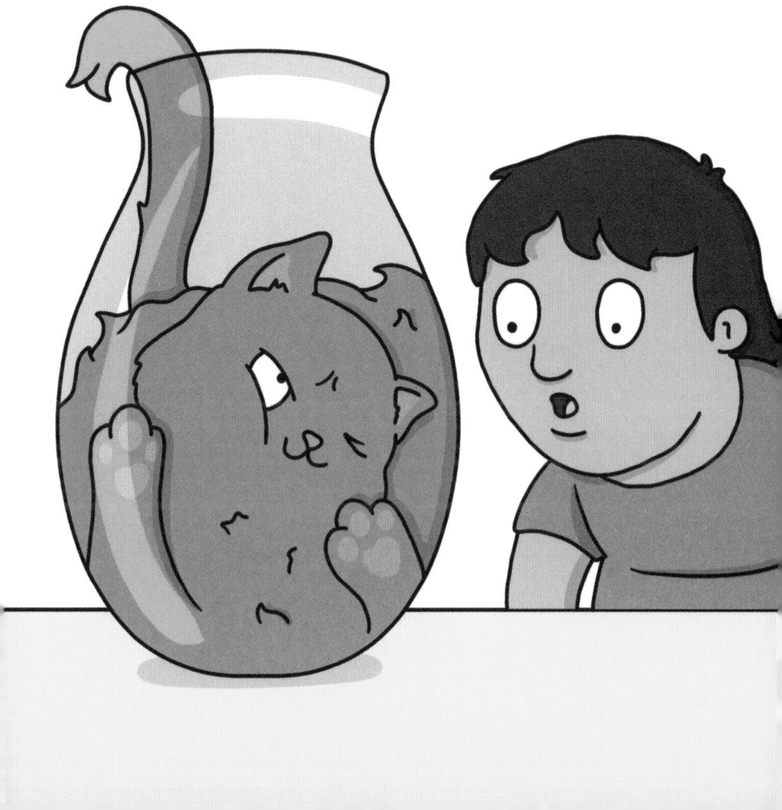

Why can't
they just pick
one hobby?

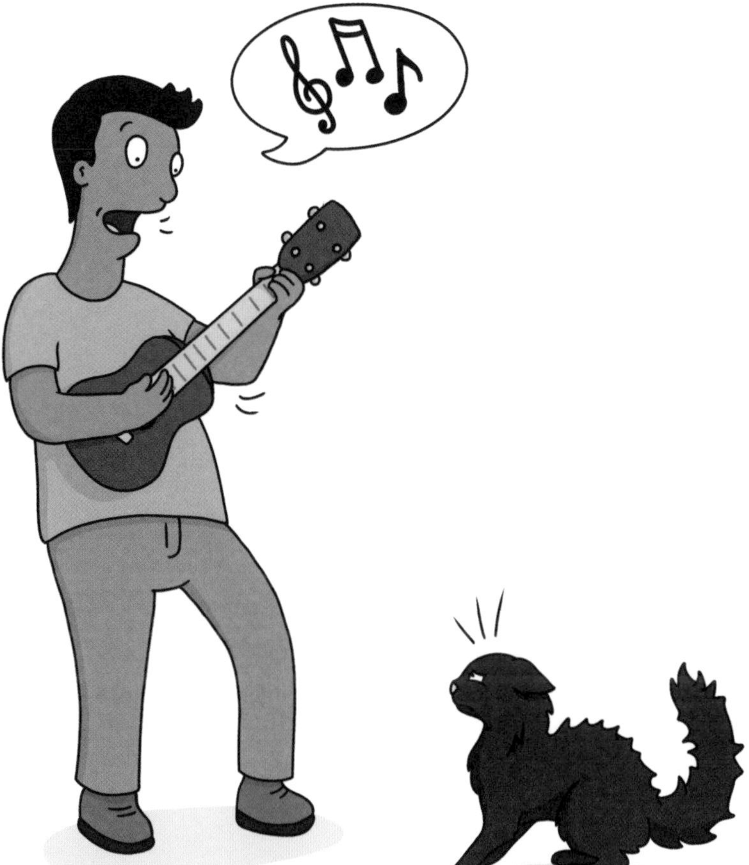

Though we'll
admit, we don't
mind this one...

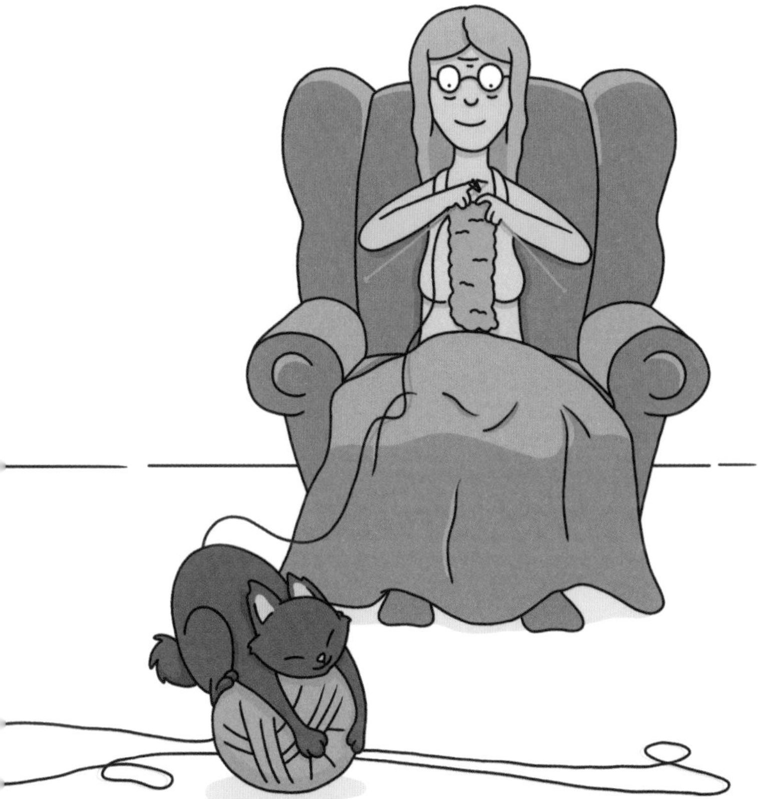

Some of their
whiskers are
questionable
at best.

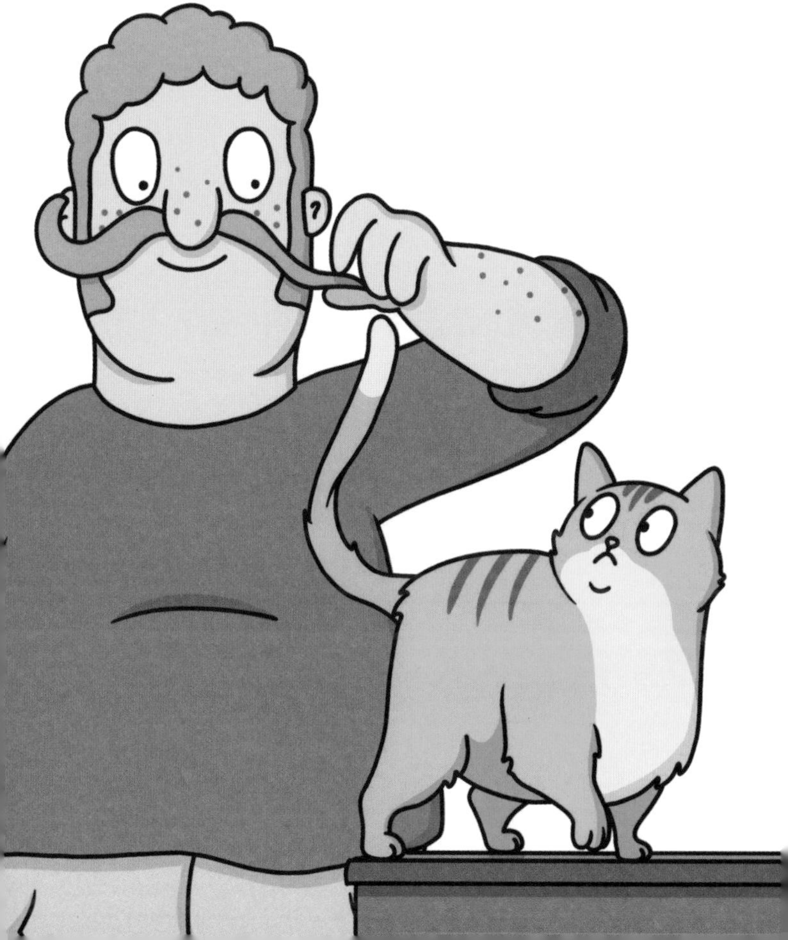

Do they not
understand that
we don't know
where our next
12-hour nap is
coming from?

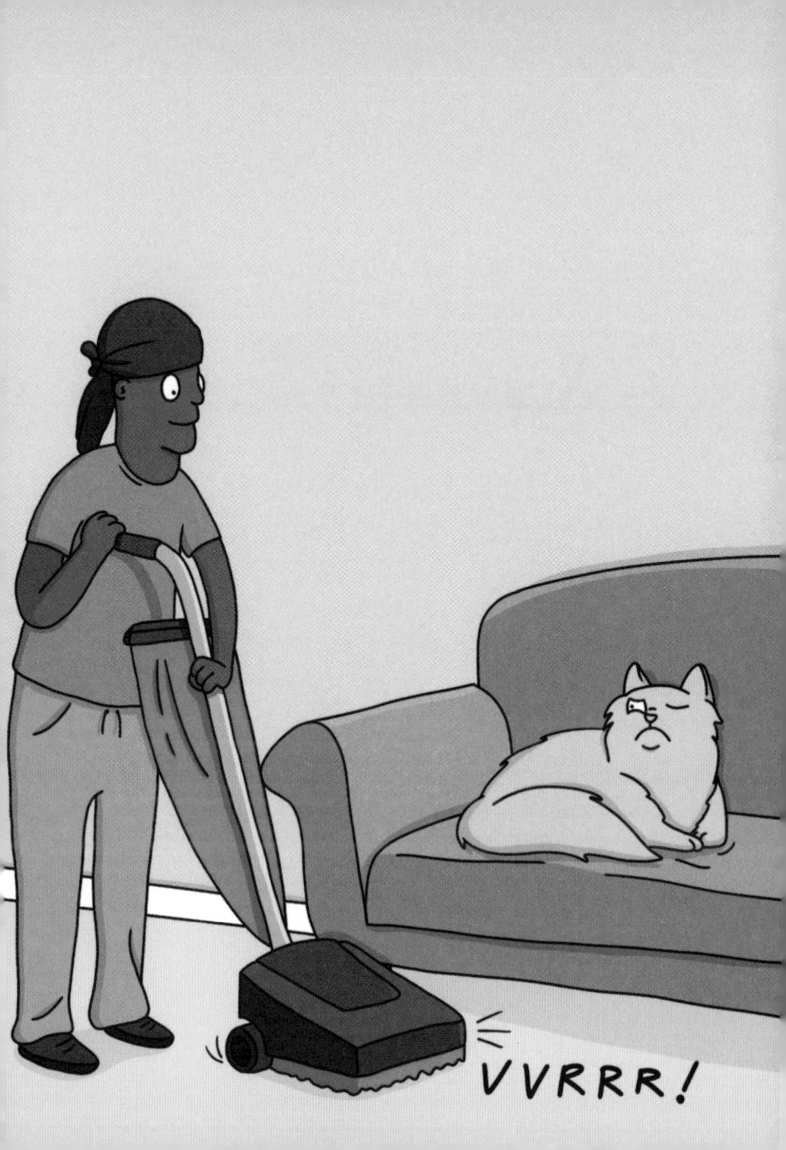
VVRRR!

Seriously? They can't think of a better way to boost their social media following?

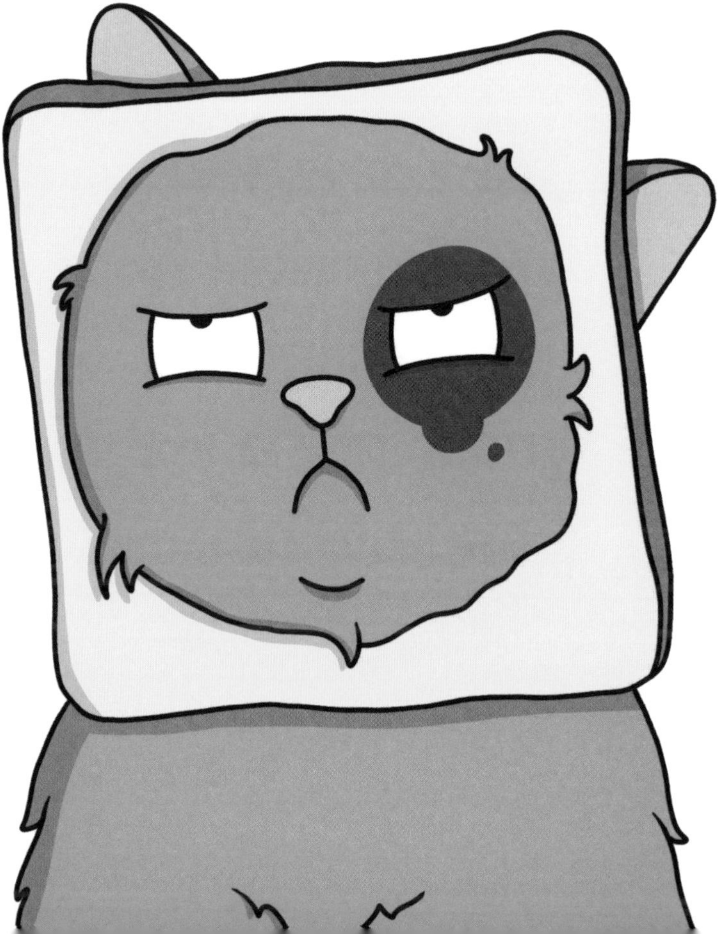

Some days, we're openly mocked for just chilling out and minding our own business.

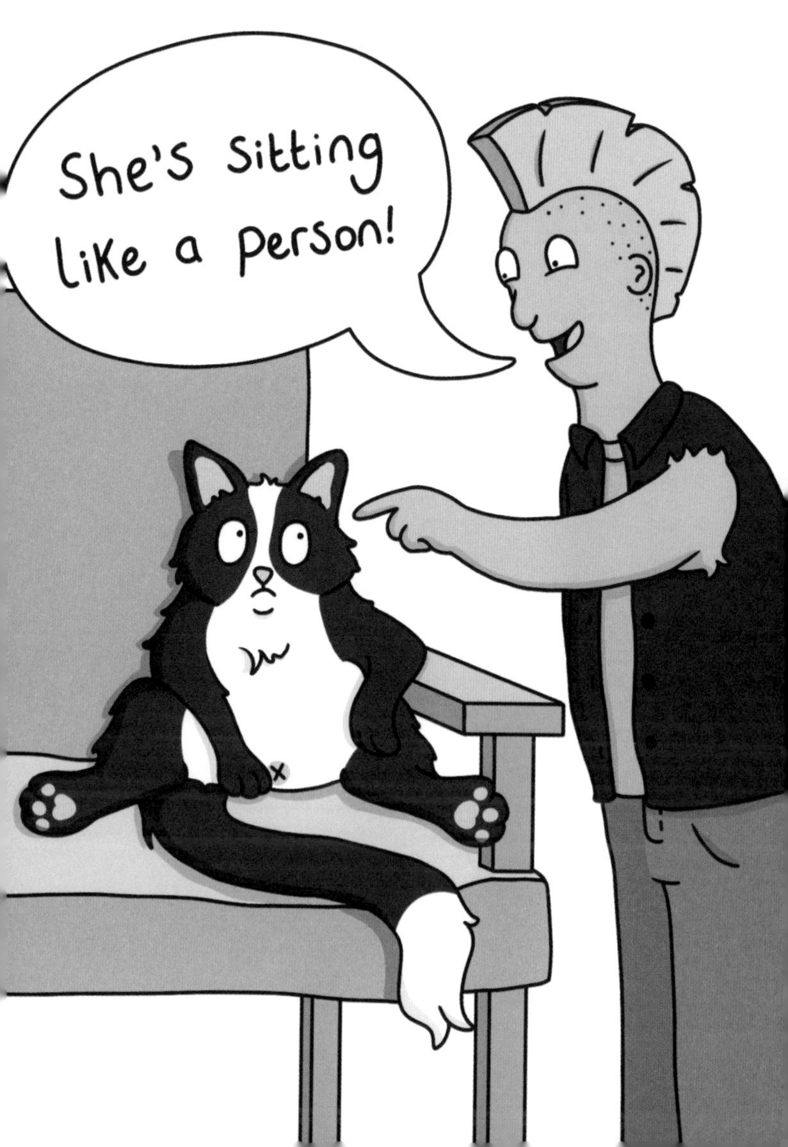
She's Sitting like a person!

They shouldn't wear such cosy clothes if they don't want us to sit on them.

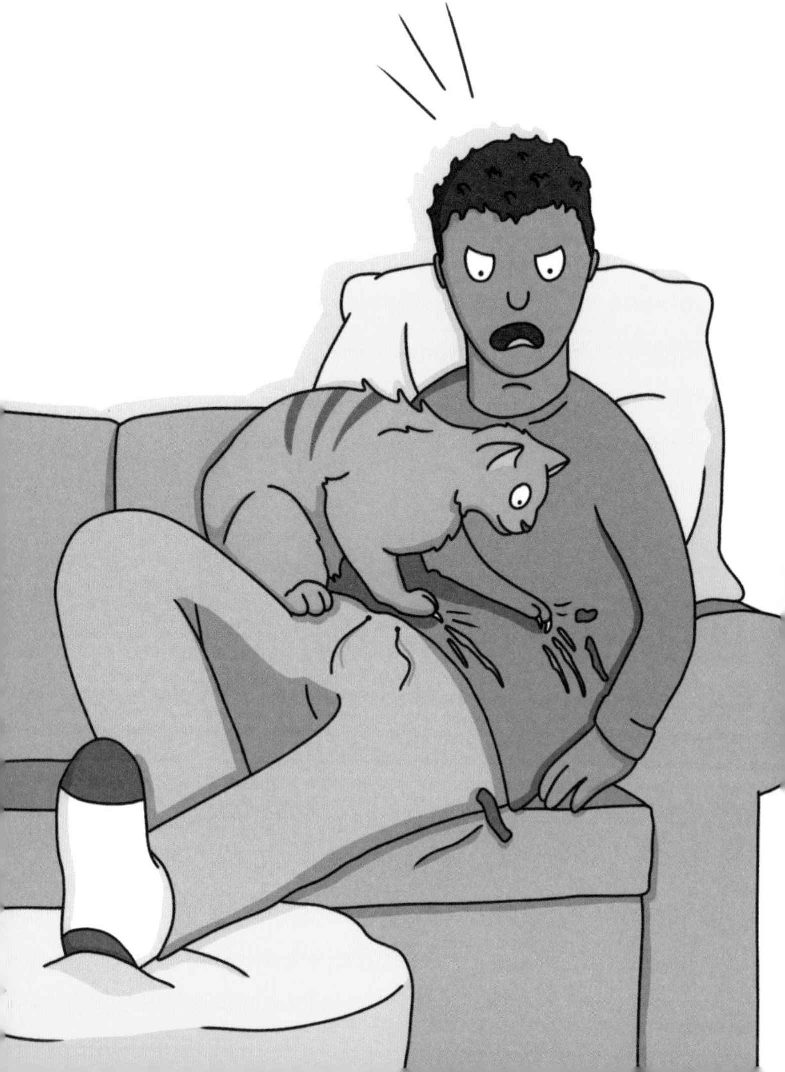

We don't know
why they care
so much about
"personal space".

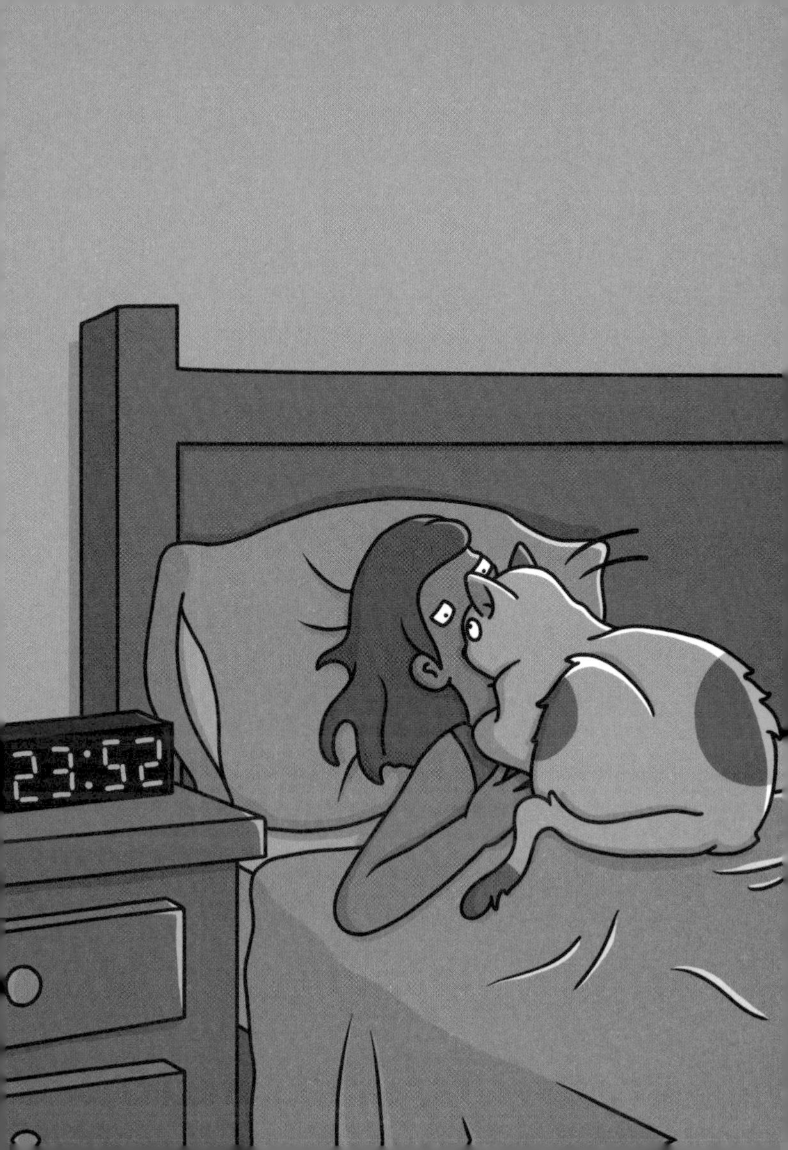
23:52

Despite their many physical advantages, they hunt the exact same thing every Friday night.

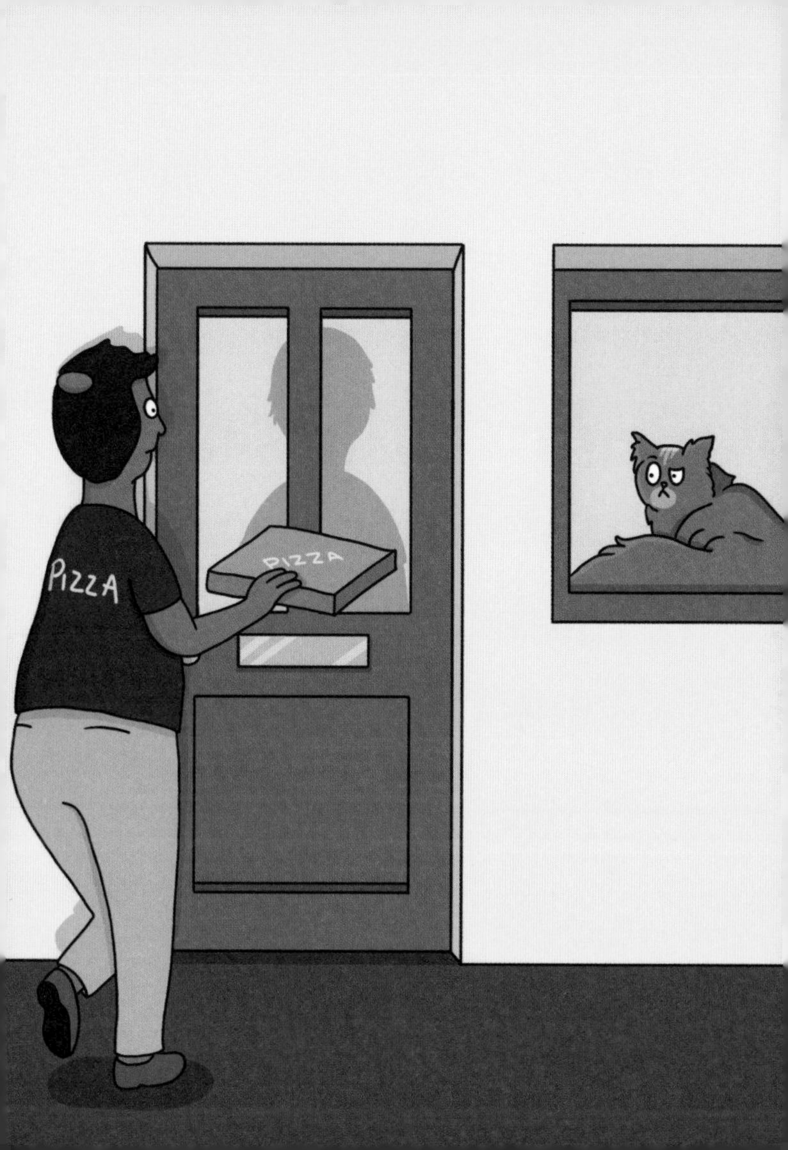
PIZZA
PIZZA

Most of the time
they only need a
cuddle. They really
are that simple!

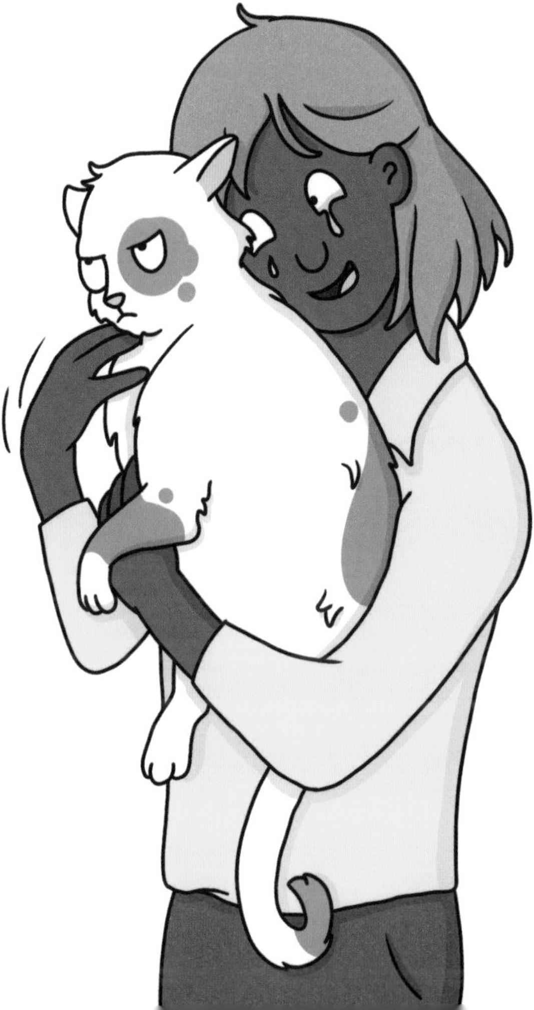

They gift us all
these scratching
posts and then
get annoyed when
we use them.

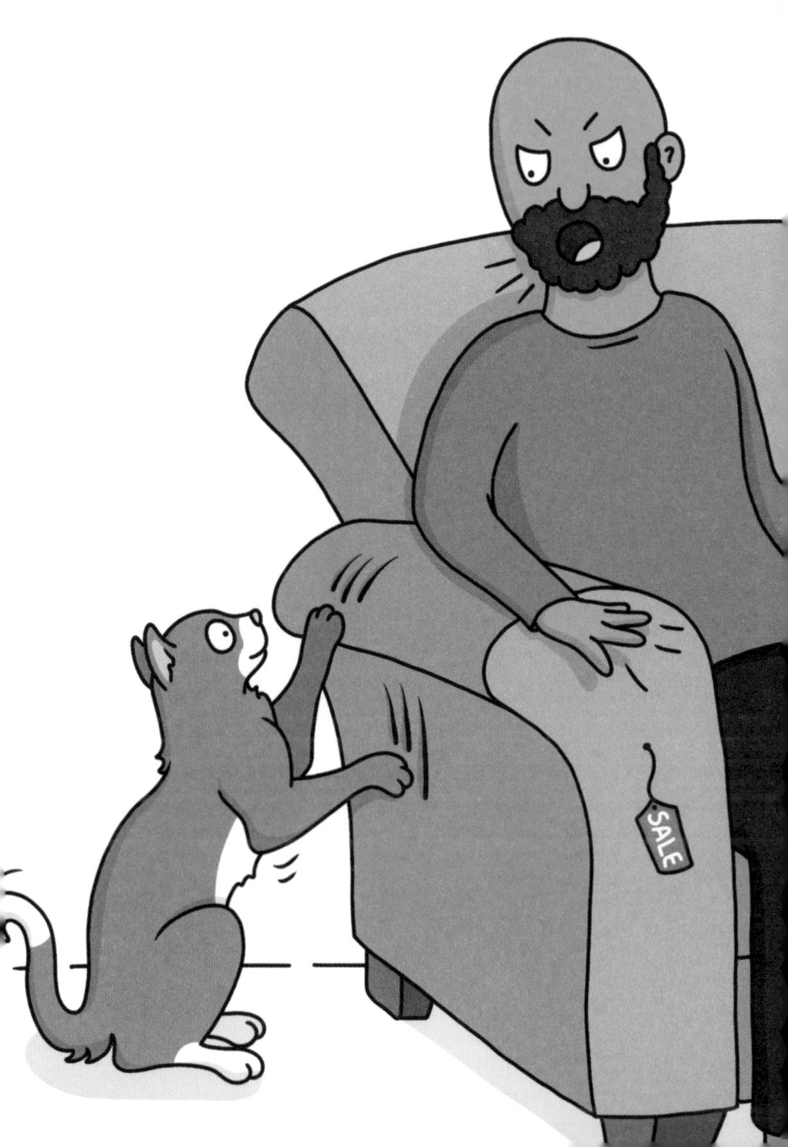
SALE

We generously create all this free insulation for them, and they just go and get rid of it.

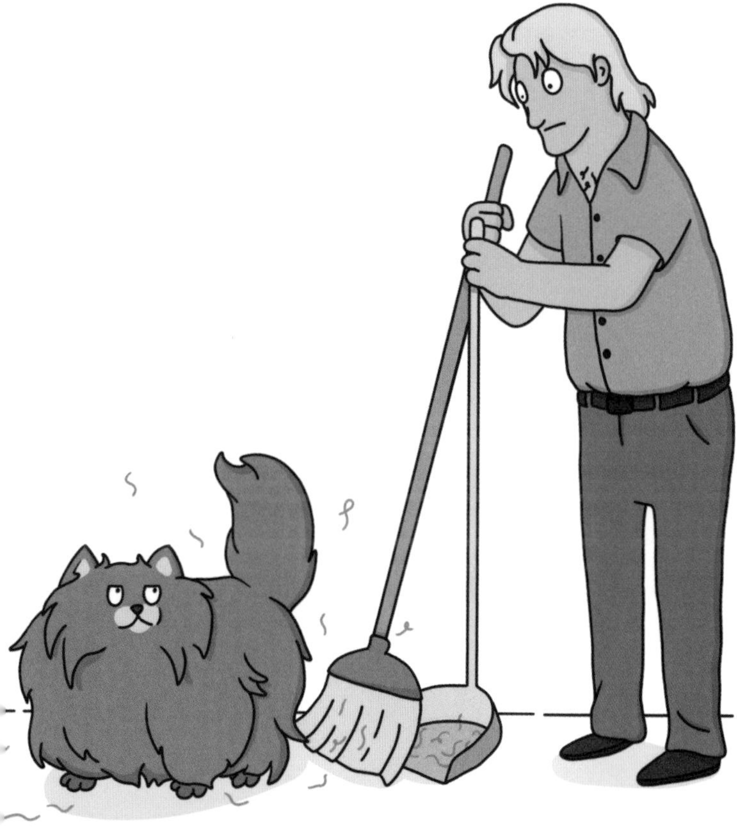

It's perfectly simple: if the day has a "t" in it and there's been a full moon in the last week, we don't want the food we had yesterday. How can they not keep track of this stuff?

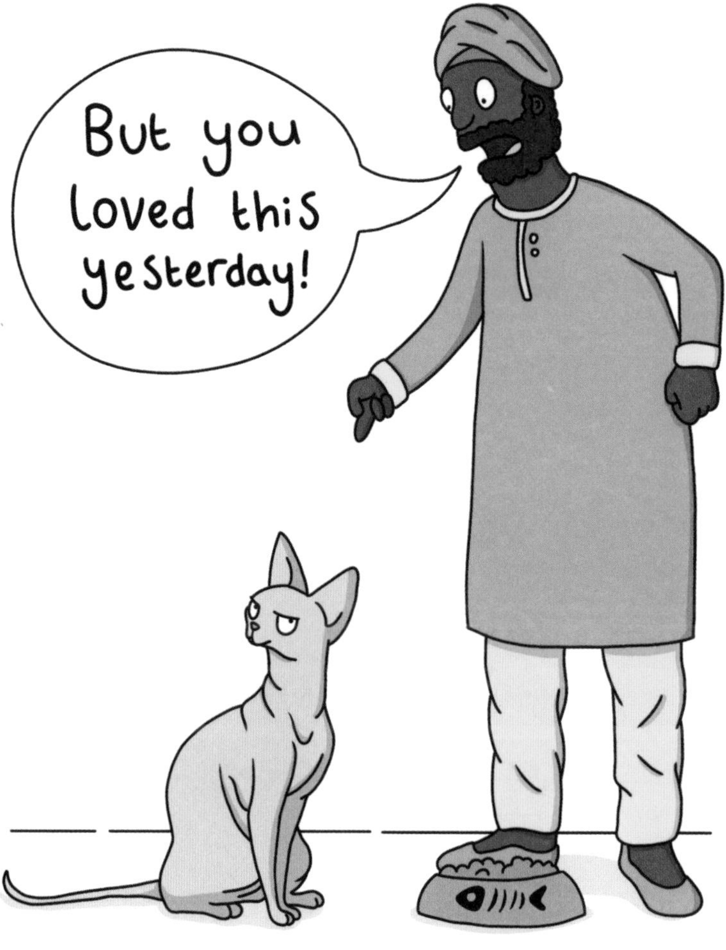
But you loved this yesterday!

Our owners are always sabotaging our attempts to be more self-sufficient.

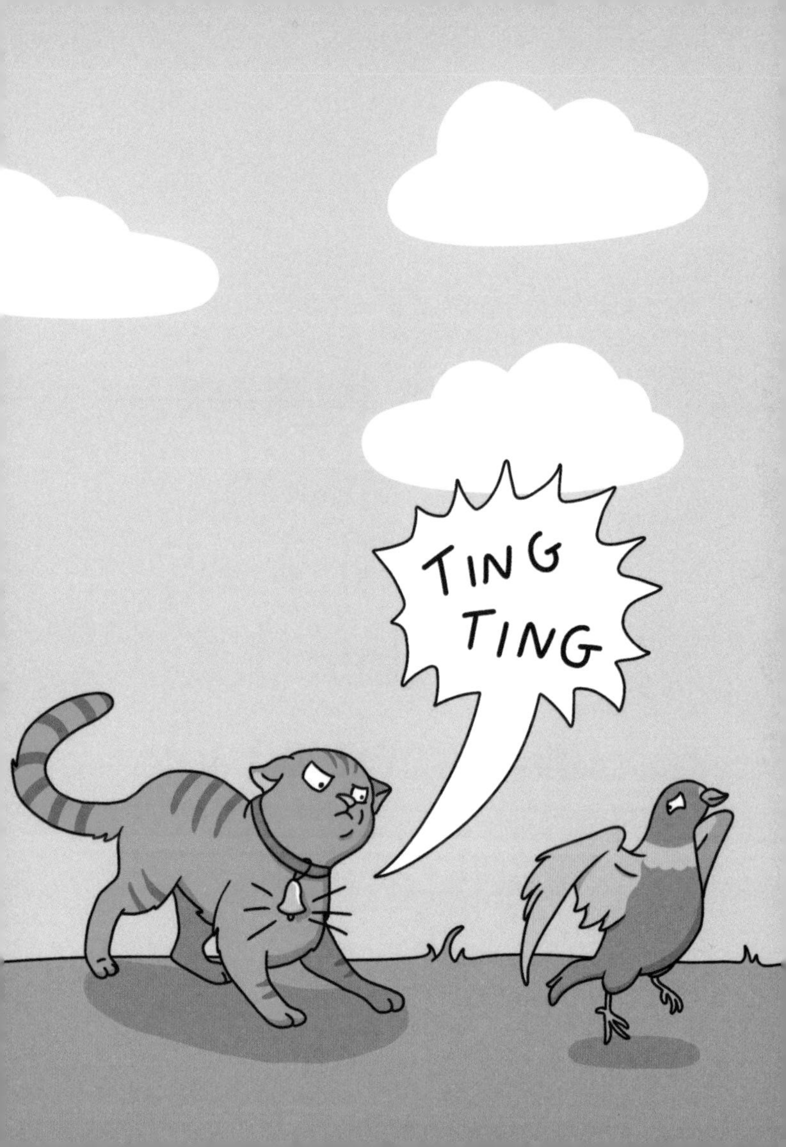
TING
TING

We are so good
at balancing,
and yet they only
remember that
one time we fell!

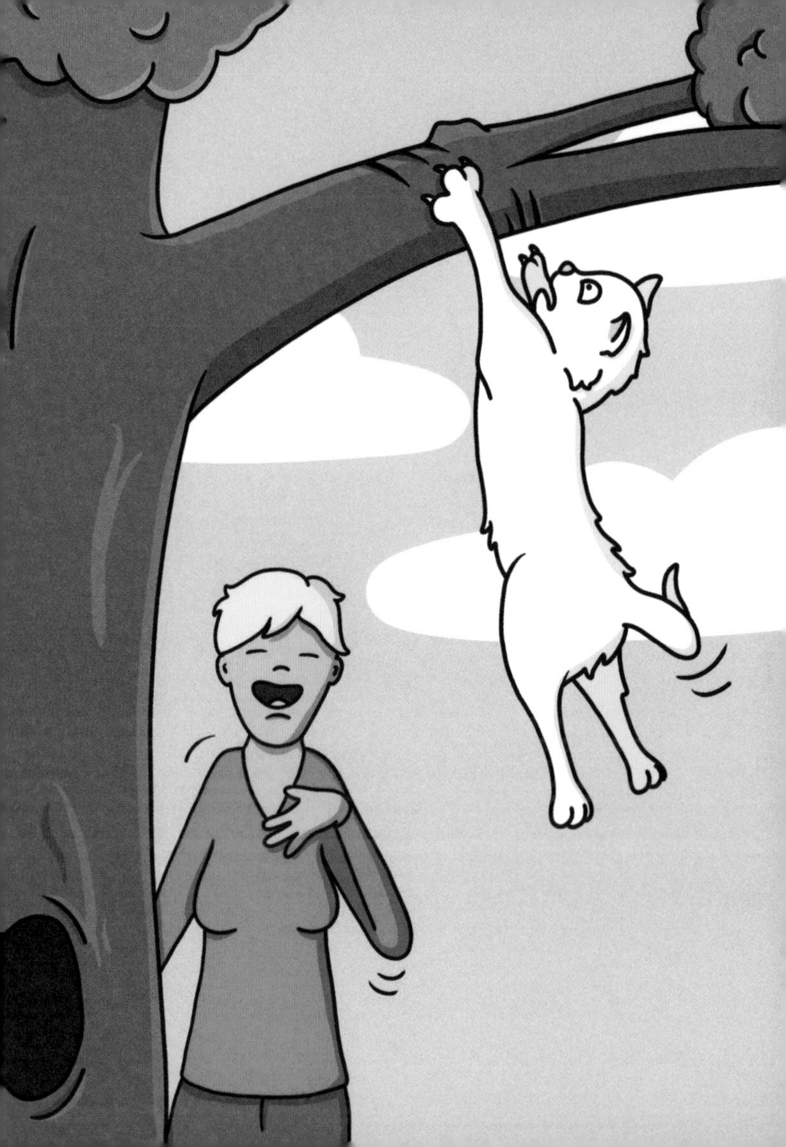

They sleep at night and get up during the day – what is that about?

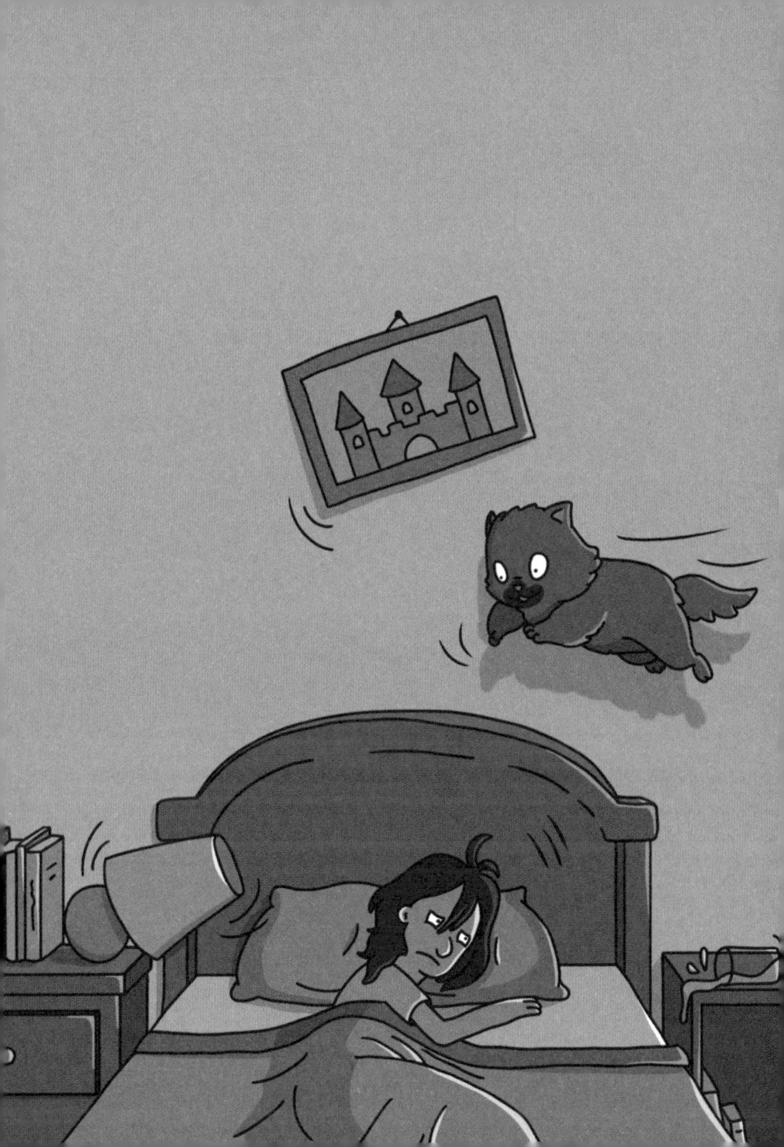

The small ones
cannot read
a room!

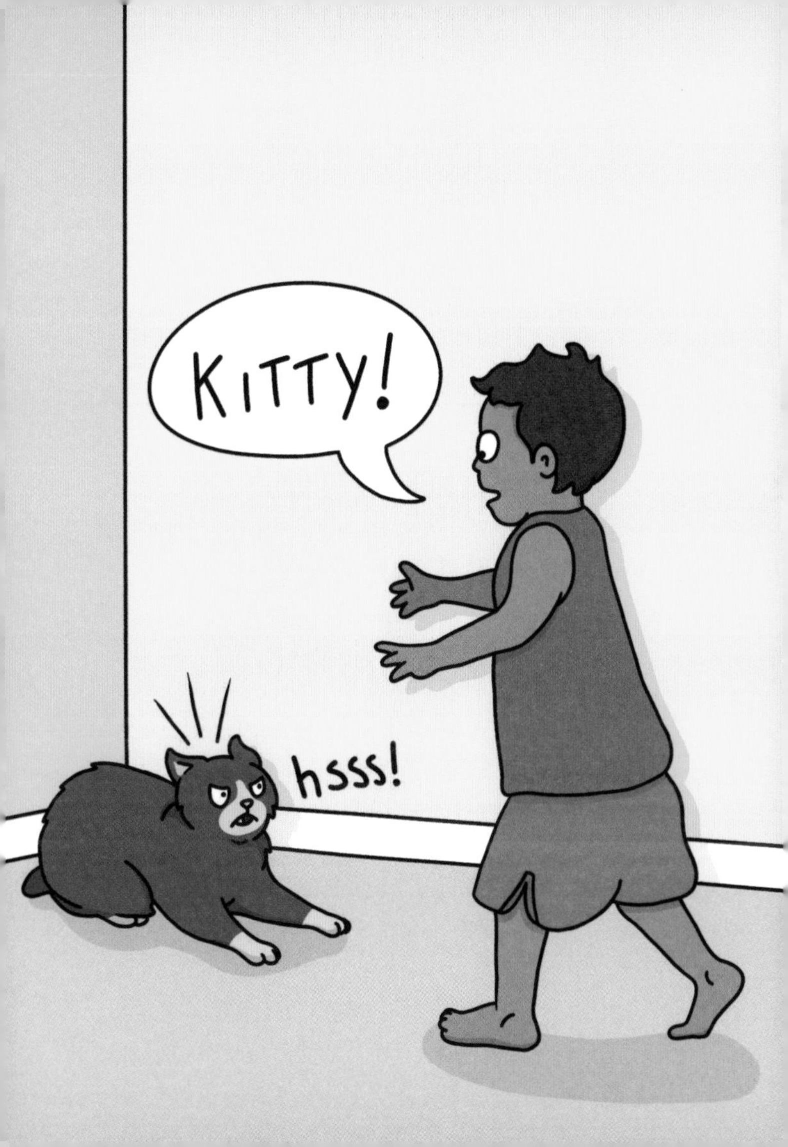
KITTY!
hsss!

They have severe
separation
anxiety and it
makes us both
look ridiculous.

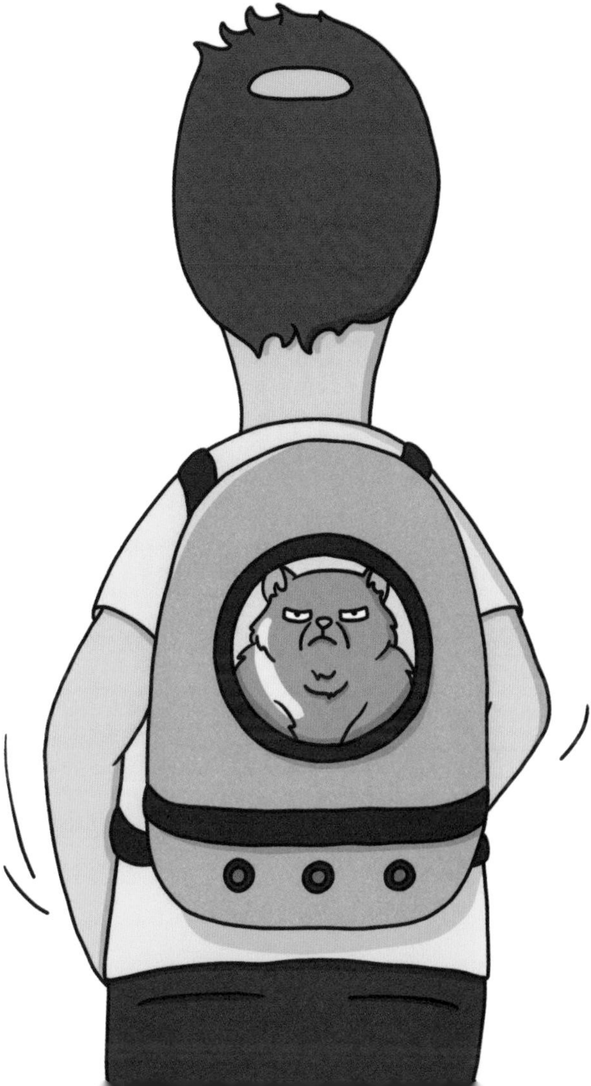

Mostly though, humans are idiots because they still haven't realized it's *us* who own them!

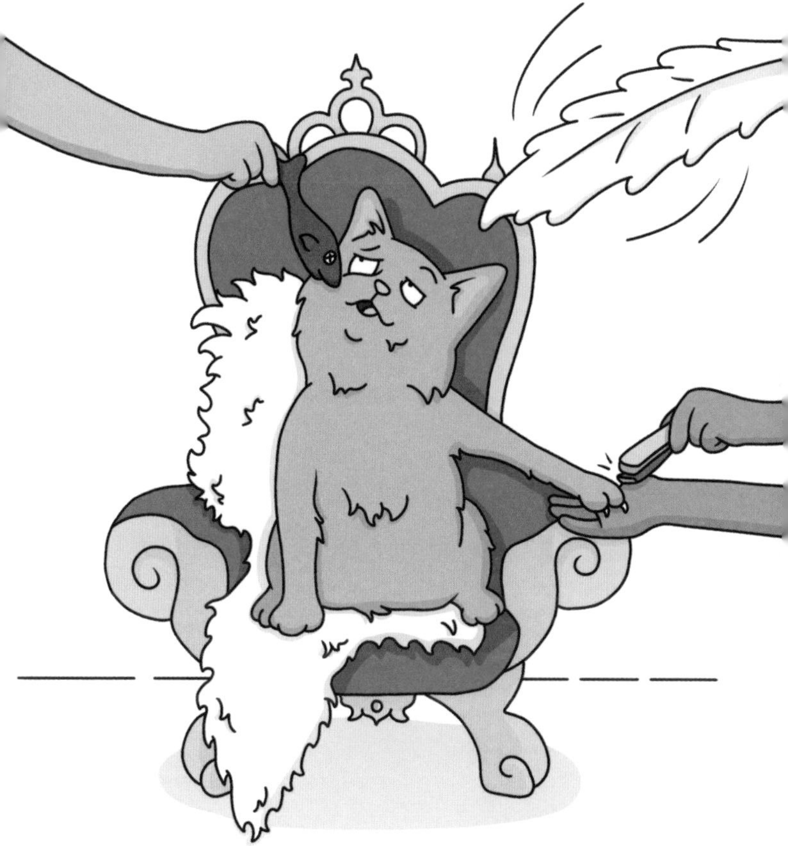

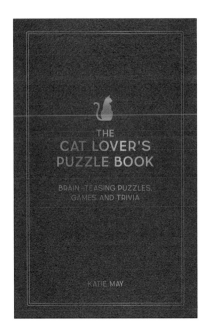

THE
CAT LOVER'S
PUZZLE BOOK

BRAIN-TEASING PUZZLES,
GAMES AND TRIVIA

KATIE MAY

978-1-80007-932-8
Hardback

When you deserve a rest from giving head-scritches, or if it's raining cats and dogs outside, why not press "paws" and enjoy a puzzle or two? From classic conundrums and quizzes to crosswords and sudoku, whether you choose to while away the hours or dip a paw in, there's plenty within these pages to keep your mind as agile as your favourite feline.

THE CAT OWNER'S
SURVIVAL GUIDE

SOPHIE JOHNSON
ILLUSTRATED BY **TATIANA DAVIDOVA**

978-1-80007-401-9
Hardback

A hilarious, fully illustrated book of tongue-in-cheek advice for surviving life as a cat parent – the perfect gift for any cat lover. This book is here to teach you all the tricks you need to help you navigate life with your furry friend, so you can focus on the positives, like giving them head-scritches and cooing over their little toe beans.

Have you enjoyed this book? If so, find us on Facebook at Summersdale Publishers, on Twitter at @Summersdale and on Instagram and TikTok at @summersdalebooks and get in touch. We'd love to hear from you!

www.summersdale.com

An Hachette UK Company
www.hachette.co.uk

Summersdale Publishers Ltd
Part of Octopus Publishing Group Limited
Carmelite House
50 Victoria Embankment
LONDON
EC4Y 0DZ
UK

www.summersdale.com

Printed and bound in Poland

ISBN: 978-1-80007-930-4

Substantial discounts on bulk quantities of Summersdale books are available to corporations, professional associations and other organizations. For details contact general enquiries: telephone: +44 (0) 1243 771107 or email: enquiries@summersdale.com.